THE LITTLE BOOK OF

THE 1980s

Published in 2024 by OH!
An Imprint of Welbeck Non-Fiction Limited,
part of Welbeck Publishing Group.
Offices in: London – 20 Mortimer Street, London W1T 3JW
and Sydney – Level 17, 207 Kent St, Sydney NSW 2000 Australia
www.welbeckpublishing.com

Compilation text © Welbeck Non-Fiction Limited 2023
Design © Welbeck Non-Fiction Limited 2023

ISBN 978-1-80069-573-3

Compiled and written by: Anna Smith
Editorial: Matt Tomlinson
Project manager: Russell Porter
Production: Arlene Lestrade

A CIP catalogue record for this book is available from the British Library

Printed in China

10 9 8 7 6 5 4 3 2 1

THE LITTLE BOOK OF

the **nineteen**

80s

retro cool and innovation

OH!

CONTENTS

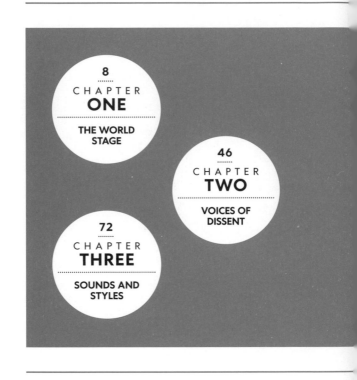

INTRODUCTION

Often dubbed the "Decade of Excess", the 1980s was a period of profound transformation. From "Reaganomics" and Cold War tensions to pop culture revolutions and tech innovations, it was a time of extraordinary cultural shifts.

As the '80s began, the intense rivalry between the United States and the Soviet Union was still very much a part of the geopolitical landscape. It was a time of heightened nuclear fears, but the policies of Mikhail Gorbachev brought glimmers of hope. At the decade's end, the monumental fall of the Berlin Wall symbolized the end of the Cold War. In South Africa, apartheid policies led to worldwide protests while the AIDS crisis gave rise to a wave of LGBTQ+ activism.

Fashion and music were at the forefront of cultural change, giving birth to iconic styles and sounds. From leg warmers and shoulder pads to the birth of hip-hop and the rise of MTV, the '80s brought us an explosion of creativity and self-expression. Literature and art flourished with unique voices and perspectives, and the silver screen dazzled with blockbuster hits such as *E.T. the Extra-Terrestrial* and *The Breakfast Club*.

The '80s was also a time of rapid technological progress, with the introduction of personal computers like the IBM PC and the birth of the World Wide Web setting the stage for the digital age. Sports played a key role in uniting people around the world, from memorable Olympic moments to the dominance of stars such as Diego Maradona in football and Martina Navratilova in tennis.

Packed full of fascinating facts and quirky asides, *The Little Book of the 1980s* will take you on a nostalgic journey through the twists and turns of this extraordinary decade. With fabulous quotes from key figures, such as Ronald Reagan, Nelson Mandela and Madonna, it's the perfect guide to this unforgettable era.

the nineteen 80s

Chapter 1
the world stage

The 1980s was a time of seismic shifts. As superpower rivalries dominated the global stage and Cold War tensions reached their zenith, the world united in the face of crises such as the AIDS epidemic and the Chernobyl disaster.

This chapter explores the pivotal events, ideological clashes and historic breakthroughs that reshaped the world order.

"

To those waiting with bated breath for that favourite media catchphrase, the U-turn, I have only one thing to say. You turn if you want to. The lady's not for turning.

"

Margaret Thatcher

The British prime minister sticks her ground, Conservative party conference, 10 October 1980

"

She has the eyes of Caligula, but the mouth of Marilyn Monroe.

"

François Mitterrand

The French president describes British prime minister, Margaret Thatcher

Reaganomics

In 1981, Ronald Reagan became the 40th president of the US. His two terms in office were marked by conservative policies, including "Reaganomics", which aimed to stimulate economic growth through tax cuts and deregulation.

Reagan's administration also focused on increasing defence spending, leading to an intensification of the arms race with the Soviet Union.

THE NINETEEN **80**S

"

Government's view of the
economy could be summed up
in a few short phrases:
If it moves, tax it. If it keeps
moving, regulate it. And if it
stops moving, subsidize it.

"

Remarks to the White House Conference on
Small Business, 15 August 1986

13

66

Well, there you go again.

99

President Ronald Reagan

A favourite phrase used during debates to deflect criticism,
most notably against Jimmy Carter in 1980

"

Honey, I forgot to duck.

"

President Ronald Reagan

Comment to his wife in the ER department following the assassination attempt on his life, 30 March 1981. He was shot in his left side.

"

It is no longer acceptable
that, while millions of human
creatures die of hunger, military
arsenals are replenished with
terrible nuclear armaments,
carriers of destruction
and death.

"

Pope John Paul II
19 March 1981

"

Pope John Paul II, a man of peace and goodness – an inspiration to the world – has been struck today by a would-be assassin's bullet. The world is horrified, and all of us grieve over this terrible act of violence.

"

President Ronald Reagan

Statement following the attempted assassination of Pope John Paul II, 13 May 1981

Fairy Tale Wedding

On 29 July 1981, an estimated 750 million people tuned in to watch Britain's Prince Charles marry Lady Diana Spencer in London's Westminster Abbey. It was a grand spectacle, but the occasion concealed a tumultuous relationship.

Although the couple were divorced in 1996, Diana's enduring legacy as the "People's Princess" and her tragic death, in 1997, would have a profound impact on the British monarchy.

"

We still cannot get over
what happened that day.
Neither of us can get over the
atmosphere; it was electric, I felt,
and so did my wife... It made
us both extraordinarily proud
to be British.

"

Prince Charles
Three months after his marriage to Lady Diana,
October 1981

Falklands War

In 1982, Argentina invaded the Falkland Islands, a remote British territory in the South Atlantic. The UK had ruled the islands for more than 150 years, and its response – led by a staunch Margaret Thatcher – was swift.

After a brief but intense conflict, lasting 74 days, British forces successfully recaptured the Falklands.

The Canada Act

In 1982, a significant milestone occurred in Canada's history with the passing of the Canada Act.

This act granted the country full control over its constitution, including the power to amend it without requiring approval from the British government.

Cold War Crisis

In 1983, Korean Air Flight 007, a commercial passenger plane, strayed into Soviet airspace near Sakhalin Island. It was shot down by a Soviet interceptor aircraft and all 269 people on board, including 61 Americans, were killed.

The tragedy resulted in one of the tensest moments of the Cold War, with anti-Soviet sentiment, particularly in the US, intensifying.

"

What civilian? [It] has flown over Kamchatka! It [came] from the ocean without identification.
I am giving the order to attack if it crosses the State border.

"

General Anatoly Kornukov
The commander of Dolinsk-Sokol Air Base during
the shooting down of Korean Air Flight 007,
from the flight transcripts, 1983

"

We affirm that a nuclear war cannot be won and must never be fought.

"

Ronald Reagan and **Mikhail Gorbachev**
Joint declaration at the Geneva Summit, 1985

Ash Wednesday Bushfires

These devastating bushfires in Australia occurred on Ash Wednesday in February 1983. Mainly affecting the states of Victoria and South Australia, they were some of the most intense and destructive fires in the country's history.

They resulted in the loss of 75 lives, the destruction of thousands of homes and significant environmental damage.

Deadly Virus

In the early 1980s, a mysterious new disease emerged, initially affecting gay communities. There was no cure, and fear and stigma grew. In 1983, HIV was identified as the virus causing AIDS – a disease that could affect anyone, regardless of sexual orientation.

The 1980s marked a critical period in the fight against AIDS, leading to eventual medical advancements, and also giving birth to an upsurge in LGBTQ+ activism.

"
AIDS:
Don't Die of Ignorance.
"

British public health campaign, 1986

Indira Gandhi

India's first female prime minister was killed by her own bodyguards on 31 October 1984. The assassination was in retaliation for Operation Blue Star, a military operation she ordered to remove Sikh militants from the Golden Temple in Amritsar.

Her death led to anti-Sikh riots in India, resulting in widespread violence and loss of life.

"

I have lived a long life, and I am proud that I spend the whole of my life in the service of my people. I am only proud of this and nothing else. I shall continue to serve until my last breath, and when I die, I can say that every drop of my blood will invigorate India and strengthen it.

"

Indira Gandhi

From her last speech, delivered the day before her assassination, 30 October 1984

War in the Middle East

From 1980 to 1988, Iraq, led by Saddam Hussein, and Iran, under Ayatollah Khomeini, were at war. The conflict, arising from territorial disputes, political differences and religious tensions, resulted in immense human and economic costs.

Despite several ceasefire attempts, the war ended in a stalemate, leaving lasting scars and reshaping the dynamics of the region.

McDonald's Massacre

In 1984, a deadly mass shooting took place at a McDonald's restaurant in San Diego, California.

James Huberty, armed with multiple firearms, killed 21 people and injured 19 others. At the time, it was the deadliest mass shooting by a lone gunman in US history.

Glasnost

In 1985, Mikhail Gorbachev became General Secretary of the Communist Party in the Soviet Union.

He introduced a series of reforms, including *Glasnost* (openness) and *Perestroika* (restructuring), aimed at revitalizing the Soviet economy and political system. His leadership marked a significant turning point in Soviet history and would contribute to the eventual dissolution of the Soviet Union in 1991.

"

Without glasnost there is not, and there cannot be, democratism, the political creativity of the masses and their participation in management.

"

Mikhail Gorbachev
The final leader of the Soviet Union

Challenger Disaster

The Space Shuttle *Challenger* exploded just 73 seconds after liftoff, on 28 January 1986. All seven crew members, including schoolteacher Christa McAuliffe, died in the tragedy. An investigation concluded that a part called an "O-ring" seal on the rocket booster had failed due to the cold temperatures.

The disaster had a profound impact on the US space programme, prompting a reassessment of safety measures.

"

We will never forget them, nor the last time we saw them this morning, as they prepared for the journey and waved goodbye and 'slipped the surly bonds of earth' to 'touch the face of God.'

"

President Ronald Reagan

In a broadcast from the Oval Office following the loss of the space shuttle *Challenger* with all its crew, 28 January 1986

The Chernobyl Disaster

On 26 April 1986, a reactor explosion at the Chernobyl Nuclear Power Plant in Pripyat, Ukraine (formerly part of the Soviet Union), released a massive amount of radioactive material into the environment.

It caused immediate deaths, long-term health effects and a widespread exclusion zone. It remains the worst nuclear disaster in history.

Black Monday

Global stock markets, including the New York Stock Exchange, plummeted on 19 October 1987. As the Dow Jones Industrial Average dropped by a record 22%, there was widespread financial turmoil and panic selling.

Regulatory changes followed, with the event serving as a cautionary example of the potential for sudden and steep market declines.

TWA Flight 847 Hijacking

In June 1985, TWA Flight 847 – carrying 147 passengers and crew – was commandeered by two Lebanese Shi'ite militants shortly after takeoff from Athens. Demanding the release of 700 Shia Muslims from Israel, the men diverted the flight to Beirut.

After a 17-day ordeal with some hostage releases and the murder of a US navy diver, international pressure led to negotiations and the eventual release of all remaining hostages.

The Great Storm

In October 1987, the UK was battered
by hurricane-strength winds.

The night before, BBC weather presenter
Michael Fish famously downplayed the
approaching storm. However, severe
weather swept across the country, causing
significant damage and several fatalities

"
Mr Gorbachev, tear down this wall!
"

President Ronald Reagan
In a speech near the Berlin Wall, West Germany,
12 June 1987

"

Read my lips: no new taxes.

"

George H.W. Bush
During his 1988 presidential campaign

The Lockerbie Disaster

On 21 December 1988, US passenger plane Pan Am Flight 103 was destroyed by a bomb over the tiny town of Lockerbie, Scotland. The explosion killed all 259 people on board and 11 people on the ground.

Investigations revealed that it was an act of terrorism carried out by Libyan agents.

The Hillsborough Disaster

In April 1989, a fatal crush of spectators resulted in the deaths of 96 Liverpool FC fans during a football match at Hillsborough Stadium in Sheffield, England.

The tragedy was attributed to overcrowding, poor policing and inadequate stadium facilities, and had a profound impact on football culture in the UK.

The Wall Crumbles

The fall of the Berlin Wall, on 9 November 1989, marked a monumental event in history. The wall, which had divided East and West Berlin since 1961, symbolized the divide between Eastern and Western blocs during the Cold War.

Signifying an end to the Cold War era, the fall of the wall weakened the already unstable East German government and paved the way for German reunification.

"

Now what belongs together will grow together.

"

Willy Brandt

Following the fall of the Berlin Wall, 10 November 1989.
Although these were not the exact words the former
chancellor of West Germany said, the pithy quote became
the motto of Germany's Social Democratic Party.

the nineteen

80s

Chapter 2
voices of dissent

From the bitter fight against apartheid
in South Africa to the burgeoning
environmental and anti-nuclear movements,
the world witnessed a surge of passionate
advocacy in the 1980s.

AIDS activists demanded recognition
and action in the face of a growing
epidemic, while artists and musicians lent
their voices to these causes, shaping a
cultural zeitgeist.

Solidarity

Led by Lech Walesa, the Solidarity movement emerged in Poland in 1980. A trade union and social movement that sought workers' rights and political reforms, it became a symbol of resistance against the communist regime.

The movement played a crucial role in the eventual dismantling of Soviet influence in Eastern Europe, paving the way for democratic changes in Poland and beyond.

"

Freedom may be the soul of
humanity, but often you have
to struggle to prove it.

"

Lech Walesa
Leader of Poland's Solidarity movement

Anti-Apartheid Movement

In the 1980s, a global campaign against South Africa's apartheid system took the form of protests, sanctions and cultural boycotts. International pressure and internal resistance eventually led to the dismantling of apartheid, culminating in the release of Nelson Mandela – whose imprisonment on Robben Island had become a symbol of the struggle – in 1990, and democratic elections in 1994.

"

During my lifetime, I have dedicated myself to this struggle of the African people. I have fought against white domination, and I have fought against black domination. I have cherished the ideal of a democratic and free society in which all persons live together in harmony and with equal opportunities. It is an ideal which I hope to live for and to achieve. But if needs be, it is an ideal for which I am prepared to die.

"

Nelson Mandela
South African anti-apartheid activist and politician who served
as the first president of South Africa, from 1994 to 1999

66

Apartheid is a crime against humanity.

99

Desmond Tutu

South African Anglican bishop and social rights activist, protesting against racial segregation in South Africa

"
An unmitigated disaster for us blacks...
"

Desmond Tutu

Describing Ronald Reagan's administration, shortly after the president's election in 1984

"

There wasn't a game in the Eighties when you didn't get racial abuse as a black player.

"

John Barnes
English footballer

"

Like racism, sexism is one of the great justifications for high female unemployment rates. Many women are 'just housewives' because in reality they are unemployed workers.

"

Angela Davis
Women, Race and Class, 1983

"

This uneasy sense of [women's rights] battles won, only to be fought over again, of battles that should have been won, according to all the rules, and yet are not, of battles that suddenly one does not really want to win, and the weariness of battle altogether – how many women feel it?

"

Betty Friedan
The Second Stage, 1981

"

Now, we are becoming the
men we wanted to marry.
Once, women were trained to
marry a doctor, not be one.

"

Gloria Steinhem
Outrageous Acts and Everyday Rebellions, 1983

Olympic Boycotts

The 1980s saw several Olympic boycotts that marred the spirit of international sport. The 1980 Summer Olympics in Moscow were boycotted by 65 countries, mainly led by the US, in protest of the Soviet Union's invasion of Afghanistan.

In retaliation, the Soviet bloc boycotted the 1984 Summer Olympics in Los Angeles.

"

I understand how you feel, and I thought about it a lot as we approached this moment, when I would have to stand here in front of fine young Americans and dedicated coaches, who have laboured... to become among the finest athletes in the world, knowing what the Olympics mean to you, to know that you would be disappointed.

"

President Jimmy Carter
Outlining his decision to boycott the 1980 summer Olympics in Moscow

CND

The 1980s anti-nuclear movement,
Campaign for Nuclear Dissarmament,
emerged in response to escalating
Cold War tensions.

High-profile rallies and civil disobedience
raised awareness about nuclear dangers,
while international cooperation,
such as the International Physicians for
the Prevention of Nuclear War, bolstered
the cause.

66

Better active today than radioactive tomorrow.

99

Anti-nuclear protest slogan

Greenpeace

Environmental movements, led by organizations such as Greenpeace, gained prominence. Protests against nuclear testing, deforestation, and pollution were common themes in the 1980s.

Notably, Greenpeace activists protested against nuclear testing in the Pacific and campaigned for the protection of whales.

66

It takes up to
40 dumb animals to
make a coat.

But only one to wear it.

99

Anti-fur Organization Lynx
Part of a campaign for Greenpeace, 1984

LGBTQ+ Activism

In the 1980s, the LGBTQ+ rights movement faced a challenging landscape. The emergence of HIV/AIDS disproportionately affected the community, leading to advocacy efforts like ACT UP.

Anti-LGBT legislation and campaigns such as "Save Our Children" were launched in the US, while the UK implemented Section 28, prohibiting discussion of homosexuality in schools. Despite these obstacles, the decade saw an uptick in activism, setting the stage for future progress.

66

The only good thing I can think to say about Section 28 is that it finally encouraged me to come out. A bit late in the day, but it remains the best thing I ever did.

99

Sir Ian McKellan
British actor and activist

" Silence = Death "

AIDS Coalition to Unleash Power (ACT UP)
Slogan used by the organization's campaign against
the AIDS epidemic, 1987

"

Activism is very seductive, and writing is painful and hard. It's very scary to have a death threat living over your head. Activism is very sustaining. But I don't view myself as a political person. I'm just someone who desperately wants to stay alive.

"

Larry Kramer
American writer and gay rights activist, who discovered he was HIV positive in 1988

The Miners' Strike

This protracted labour dispute between the National Union of Mineworkers (NUM) and Margaret Thatcher's government, over proposed coal mine closures, began on 6 March 1984.

The strike, which lasted a year, was marked by intense social tensions, violence and numerous clashes between miners and the police.

"

I never tire of paying tribute to our young miners, whose courage and determination throughout the months' battle remain an inspiration to us all.

"

Arthur Scargill

The leader of the National Union of Mineworkers (NUM) praises the resilience of striking miners, 1985

The Velvet Revolution

This peaceful and transformative series of events in Czechoslovakia, in late 1989, culminated in the overthrow of the communist regime. It was led by Václav Havel and other dissidents, with mass protests and strikes demanding democratic reforms sweeping the country.

The communist government ultimately capitulated, and Havel became the country's president.

"

The kind of hope that I often think about... I understand above all as a state of mind, not a state of the world. Either we have hope within us, or we don't... Hope is not the conviction that something will turn out well, but the certainty that something makes sense, regardless of how it turns out.

"

Václav Havel

Czech poet and playwright, who would go on to serve as the last president of Czechoslovakia, from 1989–92, and the first president of the Czech Republic, from 1993–2003

the nineteen

80s

Chapter 3

sounds and styles

The '80s were a vibrant era for both music and fashion. The decade witnessed the rise of new wave, hip-hop and glam metal, while stars such as Madonna and Prince became pop culture icons.

In an era marked by bold colours, oversized accessories and big hair, music and fashion became inextricably linked, with music videos reflecting trends and shaping the cultural landscape.

Death of an Icon

On 8 December 1980, legendary Beatles singer John Lennon was tragically shot and killed in New York City by Mark David Chapman.

His untimely death, at the age of 40, shocked the world and left an enduring void in the music industry.

"

We've got this gift of love, but
love is like a precious plant...
You've got to keep watering it.
You've got to really look after
it and nurture it.

"

John Lennon

Speaking in the months before his death in 1980

MTV

The 1980s marked the meteoric rise of MTV (Music Television). Launched in 1981, it revolutionized the music industry by popularizing music videos and providing a platform for artists to showcase their creativity visually.

Shaping fashion, music trends and youth culture, MTV transformed how music was promoted and consumed.

"

The world's first 24-hour stereo video music channel.

"

MTV's tagline, 1981

Concert in Central Park

In September 1981, the iconic folk-rock duo Simon & Garfunkel performed at an historic free concert in Central Park, New York City. The pair hadn't performed together for a decade.

The event – attended by over half a million fans – showcased timeless hits such as "Mrs Robinson" and "Bridge Over Troubled Water".

"
Beautifully articulated,
in near-perfect harmony.
"

Rolling Stone
From a review of Simon & Garfunkel's album
The Concert in Central Park

Bob Marley

In 1981, the iconic reggae musician passed away at the age of 36, succumbing to the skin cancer that had originated in his toe. Despite his relatively short life, the star left an indelible mark on the world with his timeless music and messages of love, unity and social justice.

"Open your eyes, look within. Are you satisfied with the life you're living?"

Bob Marley

Jamaican singer and songwriter

The King of Pop

With the release of his album *Thriller* in 1982, Michael Jackson became an international sensation, producing chart-topping hits such as "Billie Jean" and "Beat It".

His innovative music videos, especially "Thriller", set new standards in the industry, while his unique style and iconic dance moves made him a pop culture icon.

Michael Jackson first showcased his signature dance move, the moonwalk, during a performance of "Billie Jean" in 1983.

It involved a backward glide while appearing to walk forward, creating the illusion of defying gravity.

Live Aid

In July 1985, this groundbreaking concert, held simultaneously at London's Wembley Stadium and Philadelphia's John F. Kennedy Stadium, became the biggest live rock event ever staged.

Organized by Bob Geldof and Midge Ure to raise funds for famine relief in Ethiopia, it featured legendary performances from artists such as Queen, U2, David Bowie and Led Zeppelin.

"

You've gotta get on the phone and take the money out of your pocket. Don't go to the pub tonight, please. Stay in and give us the money. There's people dying now so gimme the money!

"

Bob Geldolf
Live Aid appeal, 13 July 1985

66

There was that 'anything is achievable' attitude in the '80s. Everything was very positive and gung-ho. Well, 'hedonistic' is the word they use a lot. We were all confident, bordering on arrogant.

99

Paul Young
English singer and songwriter

"

It was R.E.M. who showed other '80s bands how to get away with ignoring the rules – they lived in some weird town nobody never heard of, they didn't play power chords, they probably couldn't even spell 'spandex'. All they had was songs.

"

Rob Sheffield
American journalist and author

"

I'm a family-oriented guy;
I've personally started four
or five this year.

"

David Lee Roth
Lead singer of Van Halen, 1982

"

I'm self-made. I always wanted to make myself a better person because I was not educated. But that was my dream – to have class.

"

Tina Turner
American singer and songwriter, known as the
"Queen of Rock 'n' Roll"

Madonna

With hits such as "Like a Virgin", "Material Girl" and "Holiday", Madonna achieved levels of influence that were nearly unprecedented for a woman in the entertainment industry.

Her provocative style, innovative music videos and boundary-pushing performances made her a cultural icon, and her influence on the decade's music and fashion is still felt today.

"

I stand for freedom of expression, doing what you believe in, and going after your dreams.

"

Madonna

Known as the "Queen of Pop", the American singer-songwriter pushed the boundaries of artistic expression

Ten Iconic Tunes

"Another One Bites the Dust"
Queen

"Like a Virgin"
Madonna

"Purple Rain"
Prince

"With or Without You"
U2

"Billie Jean"
Michael Jackson

"Wake Me Up Before You Go-Go"
Wham!

"Sweet Child o' Mine"
Guns N' Roses

"Once in a Lifetime"
Talking Heads

"Everybody Wants to Rule the World"
Tears for Fears

"Just Like Heaven"
The Cure

"
Sex? I'd rather have a nice cup of tea.
"

Boy George
Lead singer of British band Culture Club

" A lot of people think I'm clinically mad. "

Morrissey

Frontman and songwriter of British rock band the Smiths

"

Some of our best songs were written on one string.

"

The Edge
Lead guitarist of Irish rock band U2

> **"**
> One more hit and we're the most successful girl group of all time. We'll pass The Supremes. Sad, isn't it?
> **"**

Sarah Dallin
Founding member of British-Irish pop group
Bananarama, 1988

Bold Trends

From padded shoulders to neon accessories, the 1980s was one of the boldest decades in fashion history. Here are some of the decade's key looks:

Power Dressing – Power suits with puffed shoulders symbolized women's empowerment in the workplace.

Neon and Bold Colours – Dazzling colours made a vibrant statement.

Punk and New Wave – The disaffected and rebellious favoured leather jackets, ripped jeans and bold makeup.

Sporty Chic – Athletic wear became fashionable for everyday wear, with tracksuits, leg warmers and sweatbands becoming hugely popular.

Pop Influence – Fashion was heavily influenced by pop stars like Madonna and Prince, featuring lace, fingerless gloves and bold accessories.

Big Hair – Styles such as the mullet and perm reflected the era's attention-grabbing, eclectic style.

Back in the Eighties, I'd buy the biggest Benetton jumper I could find and would wear it long-sleeved, hanging off my shoulders, with a varsity jacket and a baseball cap on back to front with a quiff. I was the smallest boy in my class, and I looked like a reject from New Kids On The Block. Terrible.

Jamie Bamber
British actor

"

My fashion was not the best in the '80s. I looked crazy as hell. I used to wear my pants tucked into my socks and karate handkerchiefs around my wrist. It was ridiculous...

"

Deon Cole
American comedian

Swatch Watches

Launched in 1983, these brightly coloured, Swiss-made timepieces were stylish and affordable.

Swatch's innovative designs and marketing strategies appealed to a younger audience and the watches became a fashion statement and a collector's item.

Jellies

Jelly shoes, made from colourful, translucent PVC plastic, exploded into the fashion world in the 1980s.

Embraced by celebrities such as Madonna and Princess Diana, they were popular for their affordability, waterproof qualities and playful designs.

The Rise of the Yuppie

Yuppies, short for "young urban professionals", were a cultural phenomenon in the 1980s. They were characterized by ambition, materialism and a flashy, consumer-driven lifestyle, and embraced trends such as power dressing, designer brands and expensive technology.

"

Hippy people had a hopeful idea of what they wanted the world to be like, then most of them changed into corporate Yuppies.

"

Patricia Arquette
American actress

Fashion Icon

In the 1980s, Princess Diana became a global fashion icon, known for her elegant yet approachable style. She popularized trends like the "Sloane Ranger" look, power suits, oversized sweaters and statement hats. Her support for British designers and her ability to effortlessly transition from formal gowns to casual attire made her a fashion trendsetter.

As the 1980s progressed, Princess Diana became more and more assured in her fashion style. Here are three iconic looks:

The Wedding Dress, 1981 – One of the most famous wedding gowns in history, Diana's dress had a 7.5m (25-ft) train.

The Black Sheep Jumper, early 1980s – Some people viewed Diana's striking sweater as a cheeky comment on how she saw her place in the Royal Family.

The Pink Ruffled Dress, 1987 – This statement gown, worn during a visit to Germany, showcased Diana's elegant yet glamorous style.

We were playing a show at Newcastle City Hall and it was a steaming-hot day and Roger had an idea where he picked up a towel, tore a strip and tied it around his head to stop the sweat from getting into his eyes. I thought it looked great, in a Jimi Hendrix sort of way, so I did the exact same. We wore it on Friday night and by Monday all of the kids were wearing it on the street.

Simon Le Bon
Lead singer of Duran Duran

"

People used to throw rocks at me for my clothes... now they wanna know where I buy them.

"

Cindi Lauper
Singer and 1980s style icon

the nineteen

80s

Chapter 4

new horizons

The decade was a revolutionary era for science and technology.

As breakthroughs such as the advent of personal computers and the Internet set the stage for the digital age, medical advancements, including the discovery of the HIV virus, had profound implications.

This chapter delves into the transformative innovations that reshaped daily life.

Round-the-Clock News

The first 24-hour cable network, CNN – or Cable News Network – was launched by Ted Turner on 1 June 1980.

CNN revolutionized television news by providing round-the-clock coverage of current events and breaking news, and paved the way for other 24-hour news networks like MSNBC and Fox News.

"

We won't be signing off until the world ends. We'll be on, we'll be covering it live, and that will be our last, last event.

"

Ted Turner
On launching his 24-hour news channel, CNN, 1 June 1980

Pac Man Fever

The iconic arcade video game Pac Man, created by Namco in 1980, became an instant success.

The game's simple yet addictive gameplay made it a cultural phenomenon, influencing pop culture and leading to numerous sequels and adaptations across various media.

The First CDs

Co-developed by Philips and Sony, compact discs (CDs) were introduced in the early 1980s. They represented a revolutionary digital audio format, replacing vinyl records and cassette tapes.

Offering superior sound quality, durability and the ability to store more than an hour of music, they quickly gained popularity, and had become the dominant music format by the end of the decade.

Artificial Heart

In 1982, Dr Robert Jarvik and his team introduced the Jarvik-7, the first successful artificial heart.

Implanted into patients suffering from end-stage heart failure, the device served as a bridge to transplant.

The first recipient, Barney Clark, survived for 112 days.

66

Leaders are visionaries with a poorly developed sense of fear, and no concept of the odds against them. They make the impossible happen. They make the impossible happen.

99

Robert Jarvik
Medical scientist who developed the Jarvik-7 artificial heart

Brick Phones

Mobile phones in the 1980s were a far cry from today's sleek and compact devices. They were large and bulky, often referred to as "brick phones".

The Motorola DynaTAC 8000X, released in 1983, is one of the most iconic early models. It weighed about 0.9 kg (2 pounds) and had a talk time of just 30 minutes.

"

Take it to work, to play, to lunch, and still keep up with your customers, your suppliers, your life.

"

Advert for the Motorola DynaTAC 8000X, the first commercially available mobile phone, 1983

Medical Milestone

Françoise Barré-Sinoussi's discovery of the HIV virus by 1983 was a groundbreaking scientific achievement. It provided crucial insights into the emerging AIDS epidemic, ultimately leading to improved diagnostics and treatments, and laid the foundation for subsequent research and efforts to combat the disease.

> **66**
>
> Female scientists should be viewed as successful according to their scientific quality, not because they are female scientists. I say to many of my students, female in particular, when you want, you can.
>
> **99**

Françoise Barré-Sinoussi
French scientist who made the Nobel prize-winning discovery
of the Human Immunodeficiency Virus (HIV), 1983

Shipwreck Discovered

In 1985, the wreckage of the RMS *Titanic* was discovered by a team of American and French researchers. The once-unsinkable luxury liner went down in 1912, with the loss of 1,500 lives.

The famous shipwreck still rests on the ocean floor, more than 3,800 metres (12,500 feet) below the surface of the North Atlantic.

"

The first thing I saw coming out of the gloom at 30 feet was this wall, this giant wall of riveted steel that rose over 100 and some feet above us...
I never looked down at the *Titanic*. I looked up at the *Titanic*.
Nothing was small.

"

Roger Ballard
Leading member of the team that discovered the *Titanic* shipwreck

PC Revolution

The 1980s witnessed the rapid growth of the personal computer industry, with companies like Apple and Microsoft leading the way.

It transformed how individuals and businesses operated, enabling tasks like word processing and spreadsheet management.

" A is for Apple.

It's the first thing you should know about personal computers.

"

Advertising campaign for the Apple computer, 1980

Forensic Science Breakthrough

DNA fingerprinting, developed by Sir Alec Jeffreys in the 1980s, revolutionized forensic science.

With diverse applications, including solving crimes, establishing paternity and identifying human remains, this breakthrough has been instrumental in criminal justice, forensics, and the understanding of genetic diversity in populations.

"

Most scientific research is a slow, painful slog, a sort of three steps forward, two steps back and the truth slowly emerges from the gloom. What we had was a rare thing in science and that was my eureka moment when we first stumbled upon the whole idea of DNA fingerprinting.

"

Sir Alec Jeffreys
British geneticist who discovered the technique
of genetic fingerprinting

Every one of us is, in the cosmic perspective, precious. If a human disagrees with you, let him live. In a hundred billion galaxies, you will not find another.

Carl Sagan

From the groundbreaking television series *Cosmos*, 1980

66

And it all came to a head when I flew, in the late 1980s, over Gombe National Park. In 1960, Gombe was part of a great forest belt that stretched across Equatorial Africa. By the late 1980s, it was a tiny island of forest, surrounded by completely bare hills... That's when it hit me: if we don't help these people to find ways of making a living without destroying their environment, we can't save chimpanzees, forests, or anything else.

99

Jane Goodall
English primatologist and anthropologist

WWW

In 1989, computer scientist Tim Berners-Lee proposed the World Wide Web (WWW) as a system for sharing and accessing information on the Internet. He went on to develop the first web browser and web server software, laying the foundation for the modern Internet.

The WWW introduced the concept of hyperlinks and web pages, transforming the way people share information and access content.

"

I hope we will use the Net to cross barriers and connect cultures.

"

Tim Berners-Lee
Creator of the world wide web, 1989

Five Incredible Inventions

These pioneering innovations reshaped music, technology, healthcare and daily life.

Magnetic Resonance Imaging (MRI)

The first clinical MRI scanners were installed in hospitals in the early 1980s, providing non-invasive, high-resolution medical imaging.

Fiber Optic Communications

Advances in this technology enabled high-speed data transmission over long distances, transforming telecommunications and data networks.

Disposable Contact Lenses

Johnson & Johnson introduced disposable soft contact lenses in 1987, offering greater convenience and hygiene for vision correction.

Disposable Camera

Introduced in the US in the 1980s, the "Kodak Fling" consisted of a simple cardboard box with a single-use camera inside.

Camcorder

Jerome Lemelson's 1980 invention changed the home film industry forever, making it possible for individuals to capture and share footage of events and personal moments.

the nineteen 80s

Chapter 5

imagination unleashed

A dynamic period in art and literature, the '80s were marked by diverse movements. The art world saw the emergence of Neo-expressionism, while street artists such as Keith Haring created vibrant murals.

In literature, authors grappled with identity, consumerism and politics, with works such as Margaret Atwood's *The Handmaid's Tale* exploring dystopian themes.

Neo-Expressionism

This prominent art movement rejected minimalism in favour of emotionally charged paintings. Artists like Jean-Michel Basquiat and Julian Schnabel were central figures, often using a raw and visceral approach.

Neo-Expressionism embraced a range of media, including painting, sculpture and mixed-media creations, revitalizing the art scene with its passionate and distinctive style.

"

I don't think about art when I'm working. I try to think about life.

"

Jean-Michel Basquiat

Leading artist of the Neo-Expressionism movement

66

Never listen to anybody when it comes to being responsible for your own paintings. It's a mistake for young artists to want to please older ones.

99

Julian Schnabel

Pioneering artist of the Neo-Expressionism movement

❝

My paintings are often strange, and sometimes show me a part of myself – a violence and physicality that scares me. It's not always pleasant or easy. I don't always like it, and really when I do them, it's a journey.

❞

Elizabeth Murray
Prominent artist in the 1980s

Appropriation Art

This movement involved the deliberate use of existing images and objects from popular culture, mass media and art history, often with a satirical edge.

It raised questions about intellectual property, the commodification of art and plagiarism. Artists such as Richard Prince and Sherrie Levine were central figures in this movement.

"

The world is filled to suffocating. Man has placed his token on every stone. Every word, every image, is leased and mortgaged. We know that a picture is but a space in which a variety of images, none of them original, blend and clash.

"

Sherrie Levine

Leading artist in the Appropriation Movement

Keith Haring

This American artist and social activist was celebrated for his iconic, graffiti-inspired art. Using bold lines and vibrant colours to convey themes of love, unity and social justice, Haring is famous for works such as "Crack is Wack".

Having used his art to advocate for AIDS awareness and other social causes, he died from AIDS-related complications in 1990.

"

I am interested in art as a means of living a life; not as a means of making a living.

"

Keith Haring

Artist in the pop art movement

Five Literary Gems

The Colour Purple, Alice Walker (1982)

An emotionally charged exploration
of the lives of African-American women in
America's rural South.

The Unbearable Lightness of Being, Milan Kundera (1984)

Explores the philosophy of love and
existence through the interconnected
lives of four characters in Prague.

The Handmaid's Tale, Margaret Atwood (1985)

A dystopian masterpiece delving into themes of gender, power and authoritarianism in a bleak future.

White Noise, Don DeLillo (1985)

A satirical novel exploring the impact of media, consumerism and fear in contemporary American society.

The Bonfire of the Vanities, Tom Wolfe (1987)

A satirical take on the excesses of Wall Street and New York City's social elite during the 1980s.

Beloved

This poetic novel by Toni Morrison tells the haunting story of Sethe, a former slave haunted by the horror of her past.

Powerfully exploring the destructive legacy of slavery, as well as themes of identity, motherhood and the lasting effects of trauma, the book won the 1988 Pulitzer Prize for fiction.

66

Freeing yourself was one
thing, claiming ownership of
that freed self was another.

99

Toni Morrison
Beloved, 1987

> 66
>
> There was a time when I thought I loved my first wife more than life itself. But now I hate her guts. I do. How do you explain that? What happened to that love? What happened to it, is what I'd like to know. I wish someone could tell me.
>
> 99

Raymond Carver
What We Talk About When We Talk About Love, 1981

"

But remember that
forgiveness too is a power.
To beg for it is a power, and to
withhold or bestow it is a power,
perhaps the greatest.

"

Margaret Atwood
The Handmaid's Tale, 1985

A Brief History of Time

This popular science book by renowned physicist Stephen Hawking aimed to explain complex scientific concepts to a general audience. The book covers topics such as the Big Bang theory, black holes, the nature of time and the search for a unified theory of everything.

It became an international bestseller, making Hawking a household name and helping to popularize cosmology and theoretical physics.

"

There could be whole antiworlds and antipeople made out of antiparticles. However, if you meet your antiself, don't shake hands! You would both vanish in a great flash of light.

"

Stephen Hawking
A Brief History of Time, 1988

It

Stephen King's 1986 horror novel revolves around the small town of Derry, Maine, and a terrifying shape-shifting entity that preys on children.

The chilling novel, which became a bestseller and remains a classic of horror literature, led to a popular TV miniseries and two film adaptations.

"

People think that I must be a very strange person. This is not correct. I have the heart of a small boy. It is in a glass jar on my desk.

"

Stephen King
American author known as "The King of Horror"

the nineteen

80s

Chapter 6
spotlights and stadiums

The 1980s were a golden era for sports, with world-class athletes such as Sebastien Coe and Martina Navratilova making their mark. Entertainment thrived with the emergence of MTV and video games, and classic films such as *E.T.* captivated audiences.

Meanwhile, the cult popularity of shows like "The A-Team" and "Diff'rent Strokes" gave rise to iconic characters and catchphrases.

Miracle on Ice

In 1980, the US ice hockey team, made up of young, amateur players, achieved a historic victory over the heavily favoured Soviet Union team during the Winter Olympics in Lake Placid, New York.

This victory captivated the nation, symbolizing Cold War tensions as well as the triumph of underdogs. The US team went on to win the gold medal, cementing its place in sports history.

"

Do you believe in miracles? Yes!

"

Al Michaels

Commentating in the final seconds of the historic
ice hockey match between the US and the
Soviet Union, 22 February 1980

Fire and Ice

In July 1980, one of the greatest tennis matches of all time took place, with Bjorn Borg beating John McEnroe to take his fifth Wimbledon title.

Borg, known for his icy-cool demeanour, and John McEnroe, famous for his fiery temperament, clashed in a thrilling five-set showdown.

"

You can't be serious, man, you cannot be serious!

"

John McEnroe's iconic challenge to the
Wimbledon umpire, June 1981

"

I was prepared to die
with blood in my boots for
the 1,500 metres.

"

Sebastian Coe
British middle-distance runner, who won the
1,500m at the Moscow Olympics, 1980

Olympic Legend

At the 1984 Los Angeles Olympics,
track and field athlete Carl Lewis achieved
a remarkable feat by winning four gold
medals in the 100m, 200m, long jump,
and 4x100m relay events. His performance
solidified his status as one of the greatest
athletes in history.

Hand of God

During the 1986 FIFA World Cup in Mexico, Argentine football legend Diego Maradona used his hand to score a goal during the quarter-final match against England.

Despite protests from the English players, the referee allowed the goal and Argentina went on to win the match – and the tournament. It remains one of the most talked-about moments in football history.

"
A little with the head of Maradona and a little with the hand of God.
"

Diego Maradona

Describing his controversial goal during the quarter-final
match against England, FIFA World Cup, 1986

Martina Navratilova

Dominating women's tennis throughout the 1980s, Martina Navratilova won a remarkable 18 Grand Slam singles titles during her career. Her legendary rivalry with Chris Evert captivated fans and helped to elevate women's tennis.

"

I think the key is for women not to set any limits.

"

Martina Navratilova
Czech-American tennis champion

80s Lingo

"Totally tubular" – outstanding

"Gag me with a spoon" – an expression of disgust

"What's your damage?" – What's your problem?

"Like, totally" – expressing agreement, often used sarcastically

"Cowabunga" – expressing surprise, brought to the forefront of pop culture by the Teenage Mutant Ninja Turtles

"Bodacious" – excellent, admirable

"Take a chill pill" – started when ADHD was first recognized and medicated during the 1980s

"That's so rad" – abbreviation of "radical", and meaning "cool"

"Wannabe" – to describe someone who wants to be like someone else

66
Roads? Where we're going we don't need roads.
99

Christopher Lloyd
In the role of eccentric time-travelling scientist
Doc Brown, *Back to the Future*, 1980

"

Life moves pretty fast. If you don't stop and look around once in a while, you could miss it.

"

Matthew Broderick

In the role of high-school slacker Ferris Bueller,
Ferris Bueller's Day Off, 1986

E.T. the Extra-Terrestrial

Directed by Steven Spielberg, this heart-warming sci-fi film – about a young boy who befriends a stranded alien and helps him return home – was a massive box-office success.

Memorable moments such as the bicycle ride across the moon and the famous "E.T. phone home" phrase have made it a cultural touchstone of the 1980s.

"

You could be happy here, I could take care of you. I wouldn't let anybody hurt you. We could grow up together, E.T.

"

Henry Thomas
In the role of Elliott, *E.T. the Extra-Terrestrial*, 1982

Five Fabulous Films

The Shining, dir Stanley Kubrick (1980)

Based on the Stephen King novel, this psychological horror film has become famous for its eerie cinematography and Jack Nicholson's terrifying descent into madness.

Ghostbusters, dir Ivan Reitman (1984)

Following a team of paranormal investigators in New York City, this supernatural comedy became a cultural phenomenon and spawned a franchise.

The Breakfast Club, dir John Hughes (1985)

A quintessential coming-of-age film that sees five students coming together during

Saturday detention, forming unexpected
bonds and challenging stereotypes.

Back to the Future,
dir Robert Zemeckis (1985)

This time-travel comedy-adventure starred
Michael J. Fox and Christopher Lloyd.
Spawning two sequels, it became a pop
culture phenomenon.

Die Hard, dir John McTiernan (1988)

McTiernan's classic action movie starred
Bruce Willis as NYPD officer John McClane
singlehandedly taking on terrorists in a
Los Angeles skyscraper.

"

I am your father.

"

Darth Vader
To his son, Luke Skywalker, *The Empire Strikes Back*, 1980

" Here's Johnny! "

Jack Nicholson
In the role of Jack Torrance in one of cinema's
most terrifying moments, *The Shining*, 1980

66
I'll have what she's having.
99

Estelle Reiner

The mother of director Rob Reiner (in the role
of a diner) responds to Meg Ryan's faked orgasm,
When Harry Met Sally, 1989

"

Carpe Diem Boys. Seize the Day. Make your lives extraordinary!

"

Robin Williams
In the role of inspirational English teacher
John Keating, *Dead Poets Society*, 1989

Top Toys

The 1980s offered a range of collectable toys that fuelled imagination and creativity.

Cabbage Patch Kids – These soft dolls with unique faces and adoption certificates were a sensation in the early 1980s, causing long queues and shortages in stores.

Transformers – A major hit with kids, these action figures could transform from robots into vehicles or animals.

Rubik's Cube – Although it was invented in 1974, this challenging 3D puzzle cube became a worldwide craze and a symbol of the decade's fascination with brainteasers.

My Little Pony – Colourful and collectible, and a favourite among young girls, these toy ponies inspired animated TV shows and other merchandise.

Teenage Mutant Ninja Turtles – Based on the popular comic book and animated series, these action figures became a huge hit with kids in the late 1980s.

Care Bears – These colourful, lovable bears each had a unique belly badge that represented their personality or special power. They featured in an animated TV series and various movies during the decade.

Iconic TV Shows

The following shows not only entertained audiences but became cultural touchstones of the 1980s:

"Cheers" – Set in a Boston bar, this beloved sitcom centres around a diverse set of regulars.

"Dallas" – The prime-time soap opera about the Ewing family's oil dynasty captivated audiences.

"The A-Team" – The action-packed series follows a group of ex-military operatives on the run.

"Neighbours" – the popular Australian soap opera was a daily dose of drama and intrigue.

"Magnum, P.I." – Tom Selleck stars as a charismatic private investigator.

"The Golden Girls" – A sitcom featuring four older women living together in Miami.

"Knight Rider" – A sci-fi action series with David Hasselhoff and a talking car named KITT.

"Hill Street Blues" – This critically acclaimed police drama revolutionized TV storytelling.

"Miami Vice" – A stylish crime drama set in Miami, known for its fashion-forward aesthetics.

66

What you talkin' 'bout, Willis?

99

Gary Coleman
In the role of Arnold Jackson, "Diff'rent Strokes"

" Lovely jubbly. "

David Jason
In the role of Derek Edward Trotter, or
Del Boy, "Only Fools and Horses"

Who Shot JR?

Airing from 1978 to 1991, with its prime run in the 1980s, "Dallas" revolved around the wealthy Ewing family's power struggles in the oil industry and their complex personal lives.

On 21 November 1980, more than 350 million people tuned in to find out "Who shot JR", making JR Ewing – played by Larry Hagman – one of TV's most famous villains.

"

Like my daddy always said, where there's a way, there's a will.

"

Larry Hagman
In the role of ruthless oil magnate JR Ewing, "Dallas"

'Dynasty' was the opportunity to take charge of my career rather than waiting around like a library book waiting to be loaned out.

Joan Collins

Commenting on her role in the iconic 1980s soap opera

"

I love it when a plan comes together.

"

George Peppard

In the role of Colonel John "Hannibal" Smith, "The A-Team"

The Simpsons

Still making its mark today, this celebrated comedy classic made its debut in 1989.

Set in the fictional town of Springfield, the series follows the lives of the Simpson family, including the bumbling but endearing Homer, his wife Marge, and their children Bart, Lisa and Maggie.

66

It takes two to lie: one to lie and one to listen.

99

Homer
"The Simpsons"

Eight Advertising Slogans

"Just do it"
Nike, 1988

"Quality never goes out of style"
Levi's, 1985

"Coke is it!"
Coca Cola, 1982

"Where's the beef?"
Wendy's fast-food chain, 1984

"**The choice of a new generation**"
Pepsi, 1985

"**The best a man can get**"
Gillette, 1989

"**When it absolutely, positively
has to be there overnight**"
FedEx, 1982

"**It keeps going... and going... and going...**"
Duracell batteries, 1989

"

I'll be back.

"

Arnold Schwarzenegger
In the lead role of *The Terminator*, 1984